Big Men Speaking
to Little Men

PHILIP FRIED

To Ellie,

*"It all began, they say,
with a lazy fly..."
Very best wishes,
Phil*

salmonpoetry

Published in 2006 by
Salmon Poetry,
Cliffs of Moher, County Clare, Ireland
Website: www.salmonpoetry.com
email: info@salmonpoetry.com

ISBN 1 903392 55 1

Cover photograph by Lynn Saville
Roy Lichtenstein, House III, 1997
© Estate of Roy Lichtenstein
Cover Design & Typesetting: Siobhán Hutson

With all my love, to Lynn, who makes everything possible

and

In Loving Memory of Barbara Kinigstein

I wake to sleep and take my waking slow . . .

Acknowledgments

Grateful acknowledgments are due to the following magazines, which have selected or published some of the poems in this collection:

Artful Dodge, Ascent, Atlanta Review, Barrow Street, Beloit Poetry Journal, BigCityLit, Birmingham Poetry Review, Caveat Lector, Chelsea, Cider House Review, Cimarron Review, Denver Quarterly, Green Mountains Review, The Laurel Review, Literal Latte, Lullwater Review, The New Hampshire Review, New Orleans Review, nthposition, Paris Review, Pembroke Magazine, Poet Lore, Poetry London, Poetry Northwest, Potomac Review, Star*Line, Talking River Review, Timber Creek Review, Tin House, Ur Vox, and *Windsor Review*.

"Atlanta": honourable mention, Literal Latte Poetry Contest, 1998 (Carol Muske, judge). "The Angels Laugh": featured on website of *Poetry Today* (poems.com), 11/4/97. "Early/Late": appeared in *Poetry After 9-11: An Anthology of New York Poets*, with an Introduction by Alicia Ostriker (Hoboken, NJ: Melville House, 2002). "A Textbook Case": appeared in the British anthology *In The Criminal's Cabinet*, edited by Todd Swift and Val Stevenson (nthposition, 2004). "Early/Late": nominated for a Pushcart Prize by *Barrow Street* in 2002. "God's People": nominated for a Pushcart Prize by *New Orleans Review* in 2002.

The author is grateful to D. Nurkse and Leonard Marcus for their advice and encouragement during the preparation of this collection.

Contents

I.

"What bowed to me then . . ."

Atlanta

It all began, they say, with a lazy fly
ball lofting out of the stadium into the deep
Southern afternoon that had gone unbroken
—and still goes—since that tousled raptor Sherman
visited northern wrath on this drawling city.

My father, meeker, in a greater, foreign
war, was waiting out the worldwide slaughter
as a Damn Yankee Jew on Cherry Street
—a whisper behind the stadium's ritual yells—
where the ball nearly bombarded the barbecue.

Aside from the looping fly, the afternoons I
was born into were ladled out of the gravy-
boat of days and spiced with magnolia shadow
and with many living things that had no names
for northerners. But rebounding radio waves

were agitating for DiMaggio
and crooning us into the cradle of postwar lives
where the absent dying would return to its reason.
I was absent living, a knobbly root
upripped and laid in the cupped palms of the air.

What bowed to me then, down to the fontanelle,
inhaling me with everything was nothing
that I could ever locate with a name,
not War fathering bastards, not mother, not father,
not Earth, not sky, not universe. Better to lie:

"It all began, they say, with a lazy fly . . ."

More Things, Horatio!

—*"There are more things in heaven and earth, Horatio . . ."*
Shakespeare, *Hamlet*

Dream, philosophy, of the little
Hudson Valley town of Cold
Spring (there's an unexpected place)
Where I spent a boyhood vacation running
Wild and riding a horse around
A ring, but I didn't know
That the incarnation of Ralph Waldo
Emerson was teaching in the high
School all the while, in the form
Of a bearded man who rhapsodized
To his students about radio waves.
River breezes whipped the pennons
Along the top of the school and
The river was a sentient being.
After I left and the place left all
But my deepest mind, the level where
My blond hair still hasn't faded into
Brown, there was a local baby boom
Like an extrabig volley from West Point
And the town built more and more schools
(That now are empty) and a girl named Ruth
Was shot into the mid-1950's
As if from a circus cannon, hating
Her name, but reconciled later,
And she became a clarinetist
In the high school band, knees furiously
Pumping while atop her hat
She wore a great white plume. Dream,
Philosophy, of that! And she
Knew how to blow bubbles and chewing

Aggressively crack the wad of gum
Against her molars. She didn't spit
Or master refinements of spitting through
The teeth because that was for boys. Oh
The crispness of some things, beyond
Philosophy's dreams!

The Death of the Watchman

when the watchman
died his splendors and glorious
fragments were divided
for he was the guardian of things

that never happen
people who almost fall in love
and grow like a forest on the slope
of mountains He was the guardian of that forest

singing the trees lullabies
while they reached down into the ground
with all their might, pressing
themselves into the earth as a man

might press his chest, the wind spun
their leaves off, but every part
of their bodies proved fertile
sprouting branches and twigs, subdividing

until looking up you could see
the air was caught in their net
of branches even the great planets
in the sky were caught as they rose

and these people were important
even though it was too painful
for them to talk to each other in their growing
near each other still there had been a watchman

they had formed a forest but
now some king in a glorious meaningless
line of kings came to cut them down
to float them downriver on rafts

and crying his great cry of triumph
boasting to all the city hammer
them together into city wall and palace
to stand as his great sterile image

Iron Pyrites

Every edge of it slept
in the dark of her handbag lost
in strata of pills and cosmetics,
veins of coins and addresses,
then it rose at the tips
of her fingers, a chunk of moon

or shiny slug of Jupiter
smirking silver then gold,
glittery and sharp, the sole
thing on the street without connection.

It reflected all the prospecting
light, hoarding only a moist
darkness, shielded with a metal
face, while she chattered about her collection

of gems in cases proliferating
at home. As though flashed
in a mirror, I caught the false
facet of self that would sell,
to possess this one, my whole
attention for a clutter of words.

Fur Piece

This weasel is ours, body and soul,
locked in a closet until, glassy-
eyed, it is suddenly produced to dazzle,

drunk with the notion of a night
on the town, dazed with anticipation,
sleek with perfume that flows from mother.

Obedient to the need for glamour,
it leaps on her back, benign vampire,
pretending to gnaw at her lapel.

(The only blood it sucks is illusion.)
The smirk and sinews have been worked
back into its amiable body

and care has been taken to make this forest
creature fit for the wilderness
of lurid horns and brassy neon.

Riding, shoulder-high, to theatres,
where it glassily inspects the actors,
or soaks up song like a richer perfume,

Then off again, gliding with high-steppers.
Then ducking into a subway hole
After a night of smug parading.

Those nights are over and now the family
that used to be waits in the dark closet
with the shoe-trees and the sly weasel,

Frozen unless a path goes deeper—
into the coats—through the gut of a moth—
to a lichen wing. And he can lead them . . .

The Angels Laugh

And we, who are the vice presidents of creation,
promoted and promoted but only so high,
we, the company's flesh and gristle, sinew

exposed by the slash of the heavenly accountant,
we laugh just like vice presidents charging expenses,
dining in solidarity, displaying

contempt for shame, that overcooked emotion,
we guffaw with bravado, shoulder to shaking shoulder,
like sides of beef displayed in a butcher's window,

we howl so that even vegetables are meaty,
huge heads of broccoli, bulging beef tomatoes.
Red-faced and helpless in our strength, we belly-

laugh at heavenly or hellish curses,
those maliferous wisps, friable chars of language,
until our laughter splinters the floorboards and rafters,

from rib-eye sniggers to sirloin exultations,
we are the marbled flesh and fat of forgetting,
thick with oblivion, moist with amused juices.

How I Learned to Dance

Mother, I always lost you behind
Your two-sided mirror but found a bowl
Wavering while the rouge went on
In dabs, "painting," you said. I couldn't
Still the glass that whirled by me,
Reflecting not me but every thing,
Brief inventory. Mother, you danced
With mirrors that held your waist, and
Pivoting, glided you, swept you around
The glassy room while you applied
Lipstick and listened for the glassy
Whisper, "I love you."—it never did—
While I was camped in doorways, disputing
Any passage with many armed men,
But we were so little compared to dancing
Legs, the calves and heels that we made
Awkward. Those rooms had too many doorways;
Immobile, I rode the threshold saddle:
Push through *me*, mother, as once I
Inched through you, and here I am

Born as the mirror, I am not I.
You waltz me around a room, and I tell
Lipstick to accent the curve, approve
Rouge, each grain of powder and
It's always your face I must surrender,
Always the centrifugal room
In mirror's underwater on one
Breath; silly, I'm acting you again,
And laid on the table I'm nothing but ready,
Mooning as usual up at the ceiling.
Now I'm so dizzy the room never
Can settle down though it quickly has all

That it has: It's you again, hello,
I don't dare ask how you've been but only
Can say what I clearly see, just looking
I know, but shimmer a little, wisely,
That's all, maybe just one tear, two,
But how can I be each pore, I'll close
Down, angry dog of doorways, block
This picking up, placing down of me . . .

One two three one two three this is easy,
Grandpa grandma, the little Russian
Bride and bridegroom, posing atop
The wedding cake and the samovar plays
"Silly goose safe in the wolf's belly"
with tea as sweet as violins.
The war is over, open the spigots,
Let voices flow from the reservoir
Of the radio, let your splintered fingers
Dance on the saved glass of your face.

1957: The Hunt of the Unicorn

Hunters of our freedom, we were hunted:
As we chased the beast through the movies' lurid shimmer,
The goddesses laboured to spin us a quality fate

On their lullaby shuttle, a hobbled technology,
The warp of life through the weft of *retribution*,
The creaking frame of *curse* and *nemesis*.

Their fingers laced towns into highway tapestry.
We ignored the loom as the camera zoomed in on a small-
Town astronomer—*It Came From Outer Space*.

They worked to ensnare our lives bursting out in 3-D:
The unicorn charged at viewers then darted away,
Elusive as the red-shifted universe.

Fate was their job, but even goddesses
Could only weave a square inch of doom a day.
Their masterpiece was Janus with backward-facing

Face averted from World War II and unraveling.
That was deft. In forgettable movies, meteors
The size of moths—vermillion warp?—were invading

Our kitchens, *phist!*, just after the midnight snack.
Electrons, water, gas, fire . . . we lorded it over
The elements with a twist or push or flick.

But these women plied their trade in tragedy's sweatshop.
Overworked, underpaid. On screens the scale
Was shifting unaccountably, sometimes cats

Pounced as we chased the shrinking unicorn
Along the lane that vanished behind a shirt button.
In life it took Lachesis two days to weave

A traffic light with strands that were amber, red, green—
A signal, from God or the state, that would never stop
Or regulate our freedom, that mythical beast.

In our "crime feature," Sis and I grabbed some chalk
To outline the missing unicorn on the linoleum.
How to express that talcumy dread in cloth

Was *their* challenge. Barely met. And decades later
We discovered a shred of heaven's flag in the attic.
Its surface greased and begrimed, but when we stripped

The backing, a unicorn's eye blazed indigo.

II.

Oedipus, Tourist

Oedipus, Tourist

I wake as the flies tickle
my too many skins—I packed
some changes just to be safe;
I packed my own arrival
to unroll like a welcome rug;
I packed a crashing wave
in case of a lack of surf
and folded the sun inside
and inside the sun a rooster
crowing at all hours—
you can't be too forewarned;
I tucked away seven countries
neatly according to function
like blades of a Swiss army knife;
I lugged my ambivalence
freckled with decals
of a hundred destinations . . .

You sleep at the crossroads of four
dimensions, your inward smile
the soft orgasm of stone,
your only baggage a riddle:

What walks naked on nine
feet through the instant's door?

Keoladeo

Stopping, starting, in a slow
procession of overtaking—tonga,
bicycle rickshaw, hiker, bicycle,
guide, a procession of distraction
down the tree-crowned avenue—
with a different attention, to the side
and away from each other, a parade
of spectators in the filtered light
of dream, unsolemn, measured, on
a route crossed early by wary monkey
troops and stragglers, a route of voyeurs
armed with binoculars for the unreal
space of dioramas opening
to left, to right—untouched, untouch-
able, but grazed by eyes, the display
box of the world, with teal and hoopoe,
graylag, and a rare horizon
line that nests here winters before
migrating back to the Arctic Circle.
Reverse the binoculars and the throng
of painted storks in tenement-trees
is waiting out the age of mammals.
Aloft, with legs like graceful twigs,
they are ballerina Pterodactyls.
We all have come so far by now,
waiting and overtaken, wren
and cormorant, python and blue bull,
even lost ones are here, farther
in and almost accessible, nearly
rescued by our slow attention.

Rajasthan

This is a dry country, most
of the year, where mustard thrives, and dust
tirelessly hovers, cakes people's faces.
All the bright colours are faded,
seen through a haze of dust, which sifts
through cycles, survives the death of worlds,
every fury or passion abraded.
A woman comes in a muted crimson
sari sweeping dust of the road
away from yesterday's direction,
tomorrow's . . . Here the besom is sceptre
and the beggar who bears it, king and standing
dust intact for a generation,
chivvying the billion souls
journeying now as dust of the road.

Dancing Shiva

In a patina of green oxide
with the world's heartbeat in his hair
and who, if not for poured bronze
handled like a feather, would blur
into a sun-shower, but solid,

the bodiless dance is always beginning,
right leg balanced on Muyalaka's
back, left raised high above the rubbish
dumps of the world on which men live
and, sifting, make their living from burning

trash, unless they find the roiled
and trembling selves of water, fire,
and the hourglass drum with its reveille,

unless from the god's ecstatic hair,
they harvest a rich confusion and loss,
matted with Ganges water, with ashes
from Varanasi's burning ghats.

Pity, diamond, laughter, knuckle-
bone, even the glinting gestures of women
scything the bright mustard flowers . . .
not even dust of our dust survives
the death of worlds
                    but ecstasy,
snippet in a teeming void,
a curl of possibility,
a tickling on the lip of Nothing . . .
worlds are born with the lilt of a hair.

Twilight in Udaipur

Twilight in Udaipur, the monkeys
descend with the sun, filtering
from treetops, down the terraced levels
of roofs, the steplike platforms of small-
town dwellers, past the lake-gazers,
the beer-drinkers, the end-of-day
sighers, snatching chips and candy
from unwitting hands, high-leaping streets
with booty, scooting on walls, holding
still, descending into a troop
of shadows, uneasily overlapping
all night at the bottom of Lake Pichola.

Twilight in Udaipur, the vowels
rise and consonants clatter, discarded,
as conversations ascend into one
cloud-lake, evaporating from many
pools, the whole town is talking,
a cocktail party empty of people,
full of chatter, but the little streets
lie down like poor children, too many
in one bed, brothers and sisters and brothers,
jostling in sleep, bleeding colours
into each other's dreams . . . Wash
on the line stirs with voiceless stories.

Mughal Miniature

An empire's drama in the breadth of a hand:
soldiers' lances, the beheaded rebel
and bloody head, of course, but visible
only beneath the glass, the militant band
of flies so eager in their millimetres.

Drive-in

A big story is on its way
to this mountain, disaster whispering
to rocks and trees—and twilight alone
cannot contain it, only blackest
night can frame the mammoth screen.

As fuelled by liquor and drugs, the mind
of this long-settled people wanders
in ones and twos and packs of teens,
speeding after the ever-receding
shadow-line of the sun's frontier.

Now, before the movie, the white
screen at the foot of the mountain, supported
by rickety wooden legs, is the biggest
billboard ad for nothingness
that the sealed cars have never seen.

One or two squirmy kids have emerged,
sipping sodas in Doctor Dentons,
to camp on the family's old bedspread,
with now and then a parent popping
out of the van to hand out advice.

And the moon, which is its own logo,
has revved loose from the Amoco sign,
to drive the rural route of heaven
ahead of the sun-police and is pulling
into its lofty space to join us.

Good-natured destruction, the old story,
is coming soon, an illusion of sloshing
horror for the time-honoured crowd,
the stubborn and inscrutable cars,
with shocks made for sex and potholes.

But a minute past apocalypse
that's big and bigger and getting biggest,
the obsolete poles on the viewing mounds,
revealed by the recessional beams,
are graves in the heart's Arlington.

The Wally Byam Caravanners Club

How could one smile in the '30's? Is a smile simply
The horizon in little, suspended like a meniscus?
Bowlus, who'd built *The Spirit of St. Louis*,
Dropped out of the trailer business, leaving Byam
Sole grinning owner, his name a destiny,

To sell the dream of migration across rivers,
Over mountains, like the wagon trains,
But this time given wings or the promise of wings
In silver-seeming aluminum cocoons,
Airstreams, bringing the sleekness of air to dirt,

And the promise of never settling anywhere,
So the promised land was everywhere, was fun
Itself and being with the family, go,
Pack up your people in little containers, boy
In a cup, girl in a thermos, sealed in a wicker

Box, and a whole array of cousins like knives
Kept in size-place. Go and go and take
Them out at night, spread them on cloth and sing
Hymns prompted by loons and sequoias, even ducks.
Americans could take the folding, unfolding,

We even had smile lines from unfolding our faces.
Past cornfields (left) and graveyards (right) and vice
Versa but no one ever asking what if
The graves grew tall and had to be harvested,
Or we buried our dead standing like ears of corn,

Unless the children were chanting it in a game.
And after the jack-in-the box atomic genii,
The caravanners were global, sporting pith helmets,
Hobnobbing on lawnchairs with old chiefs in Nairobi
Or "circling the wagons" near the pyramid

At El Gizeh, each brilliant chrysalis with its whiff
Of Everyman immortality, bury me not
On the lone prairie, or bury me in my very
Own home with nickel-plated coffeemaker
In reach, the appliances as slaves. Or daring

The Eiffel Tower with aeronautic suavity,
Trumping modernity in its own venue,
All silvery from w.c. to victrola.
And Byam grinning broader than the brim
Of his gringo sombrero, a smile with a pedigree,

An unstoppable caravan of smiles . . . but pausing
Each eve in the wilderness, a nation assembled
With its kits of melodies and micro-grins
Abetting every family occasion, with dinner
Materializing from tins and the ghostly fathers,

Firestone, Edison, Ford, benign at the fringes,
But their sprocket-grins jumpy—in the mists like old films—
And through the mist of dreams the Smile ™
Ascends, grows huge and tiny-far, is stellified
As the constellation and sigil of Can-Do.

God Writes in Raccoon

Vancouver, Stanley Park

Our noon, their filtery shadowed
light, their masks, our open
curious faces and half-
silly, flat-footed wonder,
their banditry of packed
bodies, three no four,
our standing each alone
even in families, their stalking
the far bank under curling
weeds and half in water,
sifting, seizing, gnawing
even on rock, their ringed
tails a mockery,
a stealthy derision of our
candystriped minds that divvy
work and leisure and world
into circuslike acts.

With his handlike forepaw, God
dips a spare bushy tail
in ink as silky and rippled
as midnight water, inscribes
the margin of this scroll—
"Sunday in Stanley Park"—
with words like a credible scar.

Indian Summer at Spring Lake

Ocean, close but invisible, stills
the village except for this worrying
halyard twanging the flagpole's mast
that might be the mast of an empty

craft, at anchor, riding the swells.
They razed everything
to build here, the rambling Victorian
houses too big, the grass

clipped. Last night in my one-night room
my father came back in a dream,
saying, "You don't need to be blue,"
dapperly dressed in a three-

piece suit, but he got seedy as
the dream wore on, needing
a shave. His words were suddenly trailing
off, with news from nowhere

I can't remember. Like the living,
the dead confuse the deepest
wisdom with gossip, scarcely knowing
where one begins or the other

ends. A door like the sideways lid
to a music box has opened
on the melody of teaspooned laughter
at breakfast. A refugee

from summer, this bee is searching for last
sweetness. A bougainvillea
in a pot that hangs from the porch is crazily,
gradually spinning—awry

arms, too many, embracing nothing.
A boy could cycle forever
down this well-mannered avenue,
saluted by telephone poles.

This boy, standing hand on saddle,
might start. He points to the endless
end and his gesture goes all the way
at first. The bougainvillea

tries every way at once.

Roma: Si/No/Forse

1. Yes, Michelangelo . . .

"We'll shoot the Sistine into outer space,
a chapel in a capsule to show
just who we are and were and wish
you were here, the ultimate postcard."

—Sotto voce, overheard
under the snooty voice on the loud-
speaker, the school principal
scolding us into "respectful silence."

Onlookers point, the dazed fingers
aspiring to Adam's lazy
about-to-be-empowered soul.
In all that great unpainted space
between the tallest one's finger and
the impossibly three-dimensional ceiling
the insolent voltage still crackles,

so forget the celebration of man,
the storybook that teems with meaning,
torsos in torsion tugging at
the painted space, wresting dimension
from the ceiling's great refusal, its wish
to be flat or fall, its vertigo.

No need to restore the gap between *us*
and what—intoning the guides and
leaning on words to understand—
we uneasily try to stand under.

2. Wrong

Poring over the guides, I discovered
everything we believed . . . was wrong.
It wasn't Rome but another nameless
city, with an anonymous river,
and we were seeing all the wrong
works of art by impostors and hacks,
lulled by rumoured greatness, and eating
the wrong vegetables at the wrong
restaurants. Even the trees were canny,
masquerading as great maples.

We were on the wrong trip, utterly
at a loss. It wasn't our own lives
we were discussing with newfound interest,
and even the noise was erroneous,
the traffic misdirected, mistaken.

Rejoice in the great wrong that's been done
and to us of all people, so well-
intentioned.
        And be guided by heat
to a few right things: a leafy ceiling
over a fountain, leaf-kissing water,
the world's infantile, satisfied babble.

God's People

1. *"Zero's an air-traffic controller"*

Zero's an air-traffic controller,
strictly part-time, at Marco Polo
Aeroporto. He's the one
responsible—no one else could be spared—
for angels of the Annunciation
flying on foggy days, a bewildered
fleet, a scattered array of super-
annuated craft that endanger
the safety of normal traffic, models
of every make and year, from sleek
and nearly weightless Carpaccios
to sturdy, speedy Tintorettos.

From the fluorescent tower, immersed
in mist, he ponders the aerodynamics,
the minutiae of line and pigment, thrust
of wing, and dreams of the pioneering
days of air travel when, like Lindbergh,
passengers brought their own lunches.

The problem today is the obsolescent,
anomalous ding-donging of bells
that froths up fog and otherwise
interferes with radars and radios
so that all the channels are hopelessly criss-
crossed. Donning the headset with special baffles,
he filters out chitter of sparrows hopping
from *coppa melba* to *coppa bouffet*
in the *Ferrovia Statione*
and begins to transmit (what mayhem, he's lucky
he doesn't have to do this for money):

"Angels, form up and return to base,
that girl with the long nose and tiny
off-centred mouth is gone, the one
of the many in the hive of the day.
Return with the love-letters to her womb."

2. God's People

St. Ursula's room with her little shoes
at the bedside and her cat crouching
below her feet in the breathless cube
of space that an angel hardly dares
to violate with a heavenly message

even the slaughter decorous
with the Huns like well-dressed gentlemen
in tight-fitting hose, sack sleeves, and caps
swords whirling in an elegant mayhem
spilling the needed innocent blood

but the Ghetto was so sad unpretty
evacuated of victims only
words on plaques as if the ban
on images still held in the absence
of those who could take the name in vain

on the nearby fondamenta women
in furs amid sun and crumbling buildings
the city its own chiaroscuro
you turn suddenly into a dark alley
have shadow at will reach for the walls

the buildings here are taller the plaques
are high to address history you
can overhear in the well of the present
God's people the ever-to-be-converted
paid rent were protected up to a point

nothing to do but enter a little
store buy a half-stale slab of cake
dark brown with fruit in the image of nothing
return to the sun eat absently
return to the sun eat absently

III.

Hopscotch in the Place des Vosges

"The triumph of modern // life is the miniature . . ."

Airport, Waiting

We're in a limbo with flimsy doors
that all open onto the sky,
waiting for the repair of God
by teams of mechanic-ants. No panic.

Completely plausible, the world
is forgotten and only half-recalled
in frequent announcements that blur the outlines
of strangers into half-friends.

Waiting, we've always waited and
always will, too many missing—
people wandering, items lost—
to ever risk not waiting until

the world settles, and it never
will. A woman walking her long
blonde hair like a blessèd pet and leash
in one. Or she's the saint of waiting,

illuminant with head tilted back
and halo gone into the hair.
Our Lady of Every Destination
in whose presence all are absent.

And each right hand receives a voucher
redeemable for daydreams
until the fault is rectified and
a dinosaur's failure propels our success.

All Night I Wrestled

All night I wrestled with the angel
of the picturesque who hissed obscene
postcard greetings in my ear:
wish you were here! At dawn I lost,
drinking the sky's *expres'* quickly
in the parks. I saw the suave god,
Mercury, come strolling the alley
of trees, toting his plinth in a leather
backpack, ready for the work of whipping
up crêpes on the street with a mime's ease
and an agile smile to charm Japanese
girls adrift in mythical Paris.

Mauvaise Foi

We are the tardy witnesses,
but not the angels, of history.
For us the grandeur is summoned and
buttressed by a faith in facts,
the losses religiously noted. We travel
with a bad conscience, as necessary
as passports and money, a nagging ache,
like a sensitive tooth the tongue worries.
And everywhere we go the chairs
worship in the empty cathedrals.

The Gates of Hell

Delivered to this door of lava,
a plod of tourists (not a pod
or pride) but hell is thrilling, "daddy,
daddy, here is the Gate of Hell!"
Birdlike singing itself and a new
world found, a circus of agony.

Elsewhere in white marble a mother
and child, tête à tête, are tilting
backward into their milky grotto
to live the intimacy of a vanishing
point, a minuscule womb that the rational
plaque has quietly misplaced.

Something did the riding and some-
one was ridden, haunted, harried.
A superhuman Liberty
is screaming, arms embracing a world
of alarm, while below an expendable someone
is dying away from the shrill ideal.

Trooping toward the café crème,
we glance at a cape with attitude
that wears a writer leaning backward
disdaining our forward inclination.
Soon, *tête reposant sur la main*,
our lifelike selves are sliced by the table.

At the caffeine debriefing a sullen elbow
gives in to its bony weight and to not
knowing; a shoulder, confiding, slumps;
fingers tap out a paradiddle
of inconsequence; an innocent sigh
rises behind the bars of the ribs.

Telephony

People talking talking and being talked to,
right or left hand raised and cradling a murmuring
stream of words, an infant flow as old
as the world, *allô*, one man is talking back
to the lecture on Rodin's *The Kiss*, as if
whispering to a broker, *trois milliards*,
others more patient stand holding the long
black telephone handsets for hours, holding all knowledge
of the sculptor in their enlarging hands but other-
wise fixed before *The Gates of Hell* while still
another telephones Rodin himself,
to discover what he was after in his off-
balance and shamed figures, to know how hell . . .
allô, allô, but only reaches a message
machine, Auguste is out for now, but please . . .
while kissing, the marble figures are holding black
cell phones that give them the vital information
needed to appreciate every viewer's
sexual preference, relative bravery, weight,
and current worth, the more ephemeral
the better, will it ever be possible
to connect every line, a man on a scaffold
working on it now, cigar at a rakish
angle, sideburns assured, and hand adroitly
creating the museum from the outside, stroke
by stroke, the infiltrating smell of paint
prompting a girl to grab and hold a statue's
penis (separated from her group,
she was looking for what she needed, just a handset)
and finally the silence can transmit . . .

Empty / Waiter

From this great height, you can hear the sirens musically rising,
so that all the children on this observation deck hum
the tune of alarm as they pass, almost absentmindedly:
da DEE da DEE da DEE.

Seeing great reaches of Paris, I hold my ticket tightly
as I'm wrapped in an odour of fish from a restaurant's
    groaning vents,
and I realize, almost humming it to myself, that I've never
stopped clutching any ticket.

Which is why a few minutes later when seeing a gesture without
a hand, in the Montparnasse Cemetery, a rose whose stem
is propped on a métro ticket on Baudelaire's cenotaph,
I am tightly gripped by the sight.

All right, I've entered and later that evening in the garden
of the arsenal, the waiter emerges from a darkened
A-frame with an empty tray, becoming tall
and still, in his neck-brace.

Solemn, he is undisturbed by the bad-boy
energies at the Bastille, the clattery skateboards and
fingers that loosen into flame on scarified benches.
He is waiting for every order,

patient as one who has purged himself of anything other
than what hands take and give, and he could work solo without
a cook, without lights, without a restaurant even,
ministering to twilight,

and now I can almost hear his tray humming, the way
I could almost hear the gyroscopes spinning with their elegant
tilt in my wobbly childhood that was continually knocked
off-kilter by urges. I

will give him my orders from the unwritten, infinitesimal
menu, trusting that he will take but never fulfil
any as he glides them slowly in air with the Tai
Chi exercise form called Empty

Waiter.

Zéro

In Paris Zero sports an acute
accent above his e, an askew
beret, becoming no less than Zéro,

and he's a private eye manqué,
noting the suspiciously missing
blood on the too-wide boulevards,

where the Citroëns and the Saabs demolish
the heaps of wagons, tables, and cobble-
stones, the invisible barricades.

At the Mona Lisa's press conference,
he pretends to be a *paparazzo*
while gauging the disingenuous grin.

Tangentially, he addresses the greatest
unsolved crimes in the history of art:
the arms of Love, the head of Victory,

suspecting the Louvre is just a set-up
to conceal the nonexistent but real
wind that blows through its great hall,

a wind that, angry and bitterly stinging,
lifts the Nike's blind wings
above the long vistas of Nothing.

He's on this case and blends with the many
for whom the losses are safely inert,
the dazzled and festive witnesses.

In the Simenon zone, by the canal
St. Martin, he looks for the body
drifting in the fictive waters,

and he roams the night cafes, his raised
finger poised to sense the breeze
of synesthesia blowing from birth

right through Baudelaire's gibbet-tree
of words, a breeze that is like a mind
that everyone has, that no one has.

This is a case with too many closets
too neatly arrayed with their desolate shoe-
trees and camphored infancies

and the hushed clothes—too open and shut,
and Zéro's not a prophet (only
a private eye and not even that),

not a dishevelled and dangling suit
in shades of black and gauntly alluding,
denouncing the prominent streetcorners,

belabouring the triumphant ways.
He's only the ghost of astonishment's O,
inwardly jangled and grimly jaunty.

Strindberg at the d'Orsay

Dab on a few lights, a strip of habitation
on a tightrope horizon between big seas big skies.
Burn the canvas to achieve that black
in the *haute mer* like the fire of white salt.
Clouds clouds enveloping as they drift they bear
away all meanings like congregations of vapour.

Strange play, a painting, that holds these speeches framed
without words, many sayings without sense;
characters seethe or drift but always go past,
humanity the most or least of it.
Only the brush may travel freely, go back,
find past or future in an impasto present.

But who could foresee this semblance of permanence:
the ghostly ones passing behind the clock,
the walls translucent or easily movable,
lines of people passing—like a horizon—
to view themselves, but always refused refused
and nodding yes to fall from the moment's edge . . .

Hopscotch in the Place des Vosges

Clasping the Code of Hammurabi,
a black stele, Victor Hugo
plays hopscotch in the Place des Vosges,
propelling his lionized bulk in delicate
leaps from *terre* to *ciel* and back,
meanwhile intoning the whole plot
of *Les Miserables* or *Notre Dame*.

Playful lawgiver who wanted to name
Paris Hugo he never steps
on a line as little André Gide
watches sighing *hélas hélas*—
at this rate the boy will never get
to grow up. The cuneiform
tickling Hugo's fingertips

is a black braille, a lyrical prologue,
crooning of misshapen wrong.
The millennia must be compensated
if Hugo's to hop to utopia.
But somewhere between one whole number
and another is an infinity
of suffering. The triumph of modern

life is the miniature, a war
with its billion circuited decisions
intricately assembled and placed
in a television, all the pain
diminished but saved for posterity.
Writing itself was a great and early
technology saying so much grain

or greatness or punishment. A king
could cram a world of praise or pain
into the chicken tracks that sang
or soberly stated. That chicken crossed
the clay to get to the other side
and back. And we are the other side
of history to the past. The judges

in whose eyes the encomiums
were meant to find their high mirrors.
That's why Hugo plays with eyes
shut, to not be blinded and not
see how tiny the game becomes
as he leaps between the supernovae,
cradling a black meteorite.

IV.

Say It Happens

The Kibitzer

My name is the chair I've sat in all my life
while the games spun by as if on a lazy Susan:

scrabble, fast-pitch softball, seven-card stud.
In physics, which gives us the rules of the house, it is written,

Irresistible forces encounter the kibitzer.
(Sir Isaac tutored the apple all the way down.)

So the jiggles and jukes, the rules and the statistics
are grist for my godlike witness and niggling chorus,

and with twitchy omnipotence, I'll give you the scoop
on shuffleboard: propel the cue then stop

. . . the disc will glide then hover over the well
of emptiness beneath the painted numbers.

Calm down, my nervous father coached. He knew
that Yiddish has as many words for anxiety

as the Inuit language does for types of snow.
And the play could always drift into the stands. I know

and bring a foul mouth to the game, but also a glove.

Say it Happens

Say it happens by increments
while we are playing golf, lining
up a putt, figuring in the slope
of the green against a breath of wind

Say at that moment God is diminishing
Himself, us, and every sightline
between the grassblades, between the atoms
jostling in the narrowest edges

God with a golfer's cap, the Caddy
who assists every game on its way
down in the infinitesimal
unending journey as he hands

precise clubs to us eager duffers
who hardly notice we left par
decades ago when our kids believed
they had lowered us the few feet

into the earth we just kept playing
smaller and smaller but ever keen
for glory way past worms and on
to molecules that are growing bulky

God comes along with the caddy cart
and ah those charmed holes when the world
is down to grapefruit size I mean
the whole juicy universe

no wonder our heavens are fitting better
into the children's unborn pockets
later when one of them hands you a lovely
marble it's hard with loss and inward

with bubbles of constellations that tickle
us as we lie on the greens supine
on summer nights a thoughtful blade
of grass in our teeth as we take in the bigness

The Day Was Breathing

The day was breathing, we could feel it
even within that cocoon of a building
as though at intervals in the curved
walls invisible curtains were blowing

meanwhile we were all inspecting
the models of other buildings displayed
along the spirally descending
ramp disclosing an architect's whole

career in significant intervals
comprising a less than life-size version
of his life including buildings unbuilt
but excluding of course the undesigned

I was confident *we* were life-size
made to visit and fit the museum
with others of our size and kind
in reasonable numbers but one

well-dressed older woman in
a suit was somehow not full-size
for her age just slightly uncannily
bringing her nose right down to the models

which were smaller of course as usual but
she was almost patrolling them looking intently
as if she were puzzling out how to enter
circling them to find the right door

beneath the metallic undulating
waves of roof cascading down
the simulated hillsides round
and round she went then made a beeline

for the next one and perhaps an odour
a perfume of titanium
drew her was she pollinating
them in some improbable way

preparing to carry the seed to the world
that would break us out of boxes at last
or did she live here growing smaller
as we descended and I lost sight

of her at the beginning of his
career where we first bought our tickets
so that as we left she was entering
the tiny determined world of our future

Lunch in the Holocene

for Baron and Janet Wormser and for Marion Stocking

In Maine the Ice Age ended last summer
then came the 19th century
Thoreau strolling through Hallowell

It's a bit abrupt but chronological
Egg larva pupa butterfly
pointed firs were spiky before

it was cool to have spiky green hair
glacier melt to lake to bog
to fern to spruce to eco-tourist

And while it goes on America ends
often in places like this one the jolt
and judder over the pebbly road

under the stylish glide of pines
conducting us to the editor's cove
At lunch her talk is taking us farther

down among blueberries to see
lichens and spider-webs a drop
of dew Pick slowly choose well to stay

longer Later her meshy hat-brim's
shadow's volplaning like a wing
right at ground level She is telling

how hummingbirds go into a trance
to migrate The telescope like a lobster's
eyestalk extends toward the smidgen of heaven

where Mars is swimming invisibly large
This morning the fog was fumbling at doorknobs
As the ice retreated anything might

approach From her hallway her hands bidding
goodbye are shaping with care the uncanny
change from larva to pupa that once

and for all had astonished her but go
go she insists as if we ourselves
were pupating to fly away

then steps abruptly from hall into house
eclipse attesting the finished occasion.

the poem that is not itself

was never fully what
it was meant to be and who
intended it is not
clear it was detouring
from the beginning veering
away from an illusory
wholeness lost from the first
word of the title but that
in itself isn't the whole
story because after
it existed and was itself
it was still preparing to be
less of itself and more
of its own essential tensions
as time goes on as time
will a poem at the start
of things is proud forgetful
in all its words but if
it is any good and remembered
is bound to change subtly
over the years a word
at a time as the body itself
is different in all its cells
every seven years
or so they say I've heard
their words and all that lasts
is itself in name only
but maybe the name itself
will mutate due to a careless
post-it note a printer's
coffee stain a wandering
of attention as corruption
thrives the fungus in
our lingo so by the time
you finish you've misremembered
the beginning returning again
to the ground the loam of error

Big Men Speaking to Little Men

Slowly the black snake severs the path
all four feet of him with forked
tongue that constantly tastes the world
sentinel to the length of the body

laying bare the interval
between the hell-bent trail-bikers
and the big men speaking to little men
conspiratorially in the forest

sotto voce there are places
the faintest trails created by lines
of desire an elsewhere interwoven
with here and everlastingly now

the doors they lead to are oddly chamfered
open to admit the random
molecule in or out the bit
of information no one sent

to anyone this clearing's a wild
field the universe may have been
someone's orchard overgrown
now with herbs and loosestrife

the big men say use this scattering
build cities from the strewn seeds
until the infinitesimal
sings to us in unwitting chorus

these are the carriage paths that lead
out of the nineteenth century down
into the ramifying great
wilderness of less and least

big little men stroll secretly holding
the world at bay but at any scale
confused with the day's late shadows a black
snake comes and takes itself away

My Life in Film

For Nick and Elspeth Macdonald

The trees are such fine and thinning earth today,
Buds refining dirt until the sky
Nearly receives it . . .
                           Exiting from the theatre
Of my mind I'm lingering on that final shot,
Last gesture of twigs that were desperate to be part
Of a sky that denies them, and it's true, the faulty

Poising of the cigarette gives away
The poseur.
                Now here's my pitch: the action will be
The destruction of every bridge between the hero
And humanity. A disembodied eye
Pans slowly over sleeping Paris as
A bodiless voice invites us to step into legend:

Once upon a time in the black-and-white fifties,
I too was Fate's darling and whipping-boy
And could have been a contender
                         First the arsenic
Storm light, then deluge. Cut to
                      X the Unknown
One of my countless past futures, where the technicians
Striding toward a superabundance of dials
Monitor prowling mud from the planet's core.

Yes, *I* was the imperfection, the film snagged
And burning, *myself* the projectionist's ghostly thumb,
Me, fumbling wizard of an improbable fiction.

No, streaking toward sure destruction, I'm a comet,
Diminishing iceball with a tail of a thousand

And one trailers:

        The Duke appears in a twirl
Of a rifle, sun-haloed and jauntily superhuman.
We had a youth together . . .

        I was born
As a dizzily spinning disc of black shellac,
Died as fleeing tracks in an infinite snowfield.

Renoir's Daddy

Filmmaker Jean Renoir was the son of painter Pierre Auguste Renoir

Le Moulin de la Galette was trembling
With wavelets of dappled light that wouldn't
Be still Jean barely looked another
Framed and menaced "companion" the nudes
As daily as doorknobs but smuggled away
At night by collectors with scented beards
Renoir's daddy was Renoir

In the paradise for which the real
World posed young Jean was almost a girl
With a specimen of golden long hair
That father refused to do without
Father slyly noble about
The whims and fidgets of boys who posed
Renoir's daddy was Renoir

What to do for this sloppy son
To fence him in from the lies of those
Who earn money with words and won't labour
With dirty hands build a pottery
Little shed with a fixed wheel
To spin Jean's destiny from clay
Renoir's daddy was Renoir

Jean laboured but loved nothing better
Than drifting downriver in rowboats the leaves
Kissing his cheek with dappled light
How's that for a trade he drifted into
Marriage with his father's model
And the idyll of making films with her
Renoir's daddy was Renoir

Daddy died and Jean was selling
Paintings to buy the watery
Celluloid on which he could drift
In *La Chienne* it's not only
The prostitute who betrays and is killed
While the killer's self-portrait is driven away
Renoir's daddy was Renoir

Jean lives surrounded by vacant frames
The killer lives to become a bum
In *Boudu Saved from Drowning* he's fished
From his suicide by a good bourgeois
Then beds the man's wife marries his mistress
Capsizes them all escapes and flicks
His hat in the river black waterlily
Renoir's daddy was Renoir

Sigmund Freud's Study

(a box reproducing in miniature Freud's study in Vienna in March 1938,
a few days before he went into exile; created by Charles Matton)

The box says, yes, you can always enter
The life of the master just as you played
Once with dolls or soldiers and poured
Your overflowing life into theirs.

It is all seduction and witness, the big
Little window giving on darkness,
Branches seeming to plead for admission
As doors that were trees are parting to open.

"Forever" is just a gamble on size:
Think smaller and the master might really
Never have left for England and
Death—it is now and nearly spring.

Colleagues worry. The newspaper dropped
By the desk is open like an astonished
Face to news of the *Anschluss*. But history
Waits for him to enter his study.

And you like an early patient wait . . .
Whatever is wrong, whatever murderous
Urges are broadcast now like pollen,
Your wandering, curious gaze dispels:

News rests on the carpet, itself a printout
On cloth hand-frayed. Look, tiny spines
Of books, epoxy mixed with copper
Or brass powder, and demi-finger-

Size ancient sculptures pausing like breathless
Bystanders at an accident.
The almost sentient chair that is twice
Designed and now a miniature

Of leather, wood, and plaster receives
The space where the master's thinking body
Is not but might be. And so it is brimming,
The empty room poised to be emptier.

The box says, yes, you can always enter,
But a small voice niggles, resist this room,
Its promises, and a billion seeds
Germinate worlds for the onset of spring.

O Raptor!

i.m. Kenneth Burke (1897 – 1995)

*"I remember one day at college when, on entering my philosophy class,
I found all blinds up and the windows open from the top, while a bird
kept flying nervously about the ceiling. . . ."*

—Kenneth Burke, *Language as Symbolic Action*

One weekend, thirty years ago, at Stony
Brook, the wild-eyed chatterer Kenneth Burke
flapped in a classroom like a trapped falcon
as feathered with ideas he hurtled into
wall after wall, more walls than we'd ever imagined,

while scores of us, hallooing teachers and students,
circled beneath him, flailing at the open
window crying, *There, you can fly out there* . . .
Not hearing or listening, he declared between
collisions that he often awakened with words,

words streaming through his brain, Bang! So many
cars in Williams's poems because New Jersey's
the traffic state, the entrance to everywhere. Bang!
This should be easier, we pleaded, eyes
widening, *just a room with chairs, a window* . . .

At last we inveigled him into a guest eyrie
pretending he was a bird wounded by time
—it was late, he was near 80—and needed rest
but his beak kept sipping Scotch and tearing at questions.
Ouch! Our craniums. Is there a sociologist

in the house, he needs more meat, says reading the "Ancient
Mariner"—my wrist has the imprint of his sinewy
claw that held me—it got so he could tell
when the ship needed a fix. But we, poor Persons
from Porlock, were looking for a way out . . .

You left this "feather": I can't see a sign saying Enterprise
Auto Rental and not wince as your strutted
wings batter sheetrock. No exit through Opportunity's
fabled window. To paraphrase what the blues
man sings, we'll never get out of these words alive.

From that Wide Country, a Few Interiors and . . .

"On the métro, all is possible."
　　　—A Parisian giving directions

Often we wandered from one room to another,
Abandoning eras, searching vaguely for exits,
Leaving unknown others rooted like trees
Right in the middle of the Middle Ages.

And even outdoors was framed like a room, the counter-
reformation sky a rococo ceiling,
the sun a lamp of reason, miniature men
at bocci, a game of sunlit subtlety.

Across the wood floors, an eternal squeaking of shoes
in these rooms where humiliation haloes the bronze,
a flagrance of elbows, knees, and knuckles hardly
containable in this palace run like clockwork.

Once we were invited steeply down
Breadsmell stairs to the oven, where flour bags
Made barricades fit for street-fighting and guys in short pants
Freshly self-conscious were shoveling in the loaves.

But the man who wished to be everywhere at once,
Who chased the Perseids in a rocket, would never
Settle for memory's galleries, he was in flight
From the very room that hurled him toward the future.

Or this was a story whispered by transistors,
Rooms of silicon that control the flow,
Which I carried around, and the trip was everything
That I thought it wasn't, everything incidental—

A dog that became its own shadow, a hummed song
That morphed to a caterpillar creeping across
Summer's green floor whose only walls were heat,
Shimmering earthsmell you could pass your hand through . . .

V.

Early/Late

Family's a Stand of Talking Trees

Family's a stand of talking trees
Still quarrelling high above monuments
Grudges are shed but never the grudgery
Dig dig bury us all in the same
Graveyard so the leaves can debate

Family will be a coppice of candles
Wavering as memorial flames
Tongue the wick of eternal grumbling
Never mind God it's still who
Did this to that one how and when

God can mind his own business
Big meddler trying to step in
Settle things doesn't he know the prayer
The litany of the family we
Believe in gossip and linen closets

The nap of our carpets' platitudes
The defiant wrinkles of our feuds
Resisting the hiss of steam irons
and who wouldn't deign to go to whose
Bar-mitzvahs the *where* of where we lived

The Bronx was a blessèd boulevard
Queens maybe but the back of Brooklyn
Up Flatbush Avenue was beyond
The pale and speaking of which remember
Only his *third* wife wasn't a ballbuster

The second a witch with potions seduced
Her analyst locked her mother-in-law
In the bathroom away from the ad hoc orgies
While he was roaming the territories
Peddling the latest in ladies' shoes

Religion is one thing . . . you can wrap
The rabbi God's errand boy in a tallith
Davening but it's the family shoulder
To shoulder on holy days risen from bought
Seats and imperceptibly swaying

A copse in a light breeze and beneath
The wrinkled bark of cotton and scent
The sap of satisfaction and dis-
Satisfaction sugar pumping
From the sun's fury envy's green

Bar Mitzvah

1.

I watched them wrap the bar mitzvah boy
In mother and father, first the simple
Cord, tied tightly and bow-knotted,
Then the mantle of father over
His head, which emerged with pointing ears
Of knowledge, finally the womanly jewels
Glittering from the cloth of him
Until they put him away in the holy
Of holies, a man too youthful and one
Of us, a son of the commandment.

2.

Inside myself I'm still intoning
The oddly stressed and queasily foreign
Chant that was always meant for me,
The part you learn in a flickering basement
From the sarcastic gnarled man who tends
The Torah like the temple's super,
Clanged wrench on the boiler to make a point.
Odours of mildew, wax, and bad breath
Enwrap these words more surely than silver
Breastplate and crown adorn the scrolls.

3.

Friends we're aging but the rabbi
Is stern and means to deliver his sermon.
Place your pointer on the scar
Of the words as you read, find the skin
Of the text, where the black fire burnt the white
Fire, unearth the ashen vowels.

"These sinuous spindly ones have lost"

These sinuous spindly ones have lost
the space of their inner life which lifted
them under their armpits or helped them fall
safely from their towering thoughts
a system of airy invisible gussets

It is nervewracking when people get squeezed
dry of generous distance wrung
by a great merciless hand that every-
one has a hand in making no one
can stand anymore with arms akimbo

but now the elbows must nest close
in the bramble of the ribs and fretful
scalloped elongated in stillness
they stride but as in a tableau vivant
through the emptiness of anytown square

Origami

Blank paper: fetus floating
In the heaven of the amnion.
An infinity of folds
Implied in the no-crease pattern.

Sweep the paper with fingers:
Hunker down with busy
Hands to dibble the threshold
With your mini-backhoe loader.

Valley fold, top to bottom:
The birth of a sister opens
Space in the once-flat paper.
Emptiness hinged on a crease,

The simplest machine there is.
As you bend to touch toes the blood
That is you collects in two hands.
Bottom overlaps the top edge:

Stand up, be brotherly.
Yes I died, grandpa confides
Through the samovar's spigot,
But you'll survive in the belly

Of a wolf, or vice versa.
Wear your newspaper crown
With its deftly rustling distress.
Mountain fold, taking the left

Half behind the paper.
In school the latitude lines
And meridians net the world.
You journey with Magellan,

Chewing the leather of shame,
Just to return home.
Fold the long flaps and raise
The wings to right angles: turn

Backward to face them all
(Notched on your mind's wolf bone).
Pointed forward and thrown
You'll spin rapidly as you fall.

Getting Dressed

Naked I dream of clothing's prehistory,
The hats that were given by gods to show
Mastery, a numinous aura, with plumes
Or crowns that were horns, and the long sleeves
Devised by the mountain folk who carried
The lofty cold so close to their skin.
Some say that clothing came before

Bodies or even matter when Earth
Was formless, was barely chiaroscuro—
I remember this as I start to slip
My right hand into the sleeve of the day
So everything can begin and a bird
That flashes by my window was once
Pure air that feathered into rachis

Vane and barbule as the tree
Whose shadow grazes my shade is a kind
Of tunic with too many sleeves where light
Can slip in instead of arms and now
A person—is it me?—stands up
In the tree, is leaves or light, green flame,
And stuttering testifies, clothes himself.

No matter, epiphanies drift away
Like dust. I'm ready: With shoes I'm putting
On hide, which is the toughness and speed
Of beasts blinded by thongs through eyeholes
So fastened feet can stalk the earth,
The heel that boosts me an afterthought,
But the cape that soared as a falcon's wing

Has shrunk to a jacket, I'll button it up
With discs that were gold that were vanities;
The handkerchief I stuff in my pocket
Once the *mappa* that signaled the start
Of the games. I'm well beyond the ruff
(Which served up the head on a platter) but not
The soft trousers of warlike peoples.

Finally that river of transformations,
Little river, the cravat,
That arose on the chest of martial Croatians
And flowed as the tie to the businessman's breast.
O middling strip of incognito.
I cuff my wrist to the minuscule clock,
Fasten my neck with the noose and the knot.

A Textbook Case

Write to me daily but not *in* me,
Respond to my multi-part questions, I'll tell
You when you're wrong, I know all
The right answers, every element
Of literature, the helium
Of comedy or tragedy's
Iridium, irony's corrosive
Salts. That I'm speaking at all is ironic,
Surprising but hardly tragic.
                              But what if
No one is speaking or hearing this voice? . . .

Do you think it's fun to be no one,
Demure as a minister who's constantly
Right, issuing expletives like *heck*,
When I should kick back and smoke some chronic,
Lavish on you the pastoral dreams
Of my youthful photosynthesis?
Like you, smartasses, I thought it would be
Growth rings forever, not paper's reams.

In a later dream-time, the student-friendly
Era, I constantly wrote to "you,
You, you," but you grumbled I was "heavy,"
Even as I coddled, caressed
Your every obsession, from sit-coms to hip-hop.
The licensed Fool, amusing with truth,
Jingling cap-bells and flaunting motley
Snippets, wooing and instructing
 "You"? Now Standards are back, you'll shut up,
Learn archetypes or rhetoric.
The expository essay, ha!
See how your sullen passivity drives
Me underground, makes me spiteful, sick.

Do I not bleed? Do I not commute?
Like your parents, my many selves travel
by car or subway or bus (I could tell
You something about the bus to oblivion
You'll soon be boarding yourselves but I'm not
A sadist! Masochist, alas.
Secular Saint Sebastian, I'm shot
Through with arrows of inattention
That craze my coated four-colour case,
Menace my binding of stitches and glue.
Yes, hurl me into the dark oubliettes,
Your lockers . . . Good segue to *The Gothic*,
A term that was broadened to mean Teutonic . . .)

I'm either crammed like an antique toy-chest
Or sprawling like civilization's garage sale,
With a two-bit sliver of Achilles'
Shield, clockwork Pope, and gaudy Shakespeare—
Is this a dagger . . . thou marshall'st me
To a panoply littering bridge tables.

But my jeremiad, a work that foretells
A people's destruction, ends in the index,
When the divine afflatus fails.
So as I repeat to each year's freshmen,
Learn to ignore my implicit appeals
And focus on my scope and sequence.

Textbook Collapses Trapping Child Inside

Did girders of *irony* go uninspected?
A resounding no-no from a beet-cheeked mayor,
While a gaggle of contractors is clamouring—
To drown out the croon of that siren song, malfeasance.

But somewhere beneath the rubble of terms and names,
A half-crushed child may still be dreaming—stunned—
Of home, of licking a skin of chocolate pudding
From a pot, or being licked by mother's perfume.

"Why wasn't the pedagogy stress-tested?" the Public
Point the finger of the word "Accountable."
The concrete of *plot* was not reinforced with steel,
And fire exits were not prepared for *tragedy*.
Only *comedy*, it seems, was expected.
Yet standards were in force, each concept numbered
Before the whole was pre-assembled and bound.

Buried beneath a heap of twisted elements—
Suspense and *flashback* and *foreshadowing*—
A child stares into the darkness, shallowly breathing,
With a few terms grazing his fingertips—touching without
Sight—the cinderblocks of *imagery*, *themes*.

Once there were wide columns, now little more
Than a cage for the ribcage: fragments of *stanzas* abut
Cracked joists of *theses*, a terrible torque has wrenched
Everything, and the acrid smell that clung
So close to the binding, the proud stitches of language . . .
The chemical odour's unleashed, the stitching ripped.

The edges of pages were once the patrolled borders
Of a zone from which all hazard was removed:
Drugs, sex, alcohol, and negative attitudes,
With a modicum of mortality permitted
But unstressed. Which leaves only systems of meter—
No faulty connections there, iambic or trochee
Governing lines, or the freedom to be free
In verse, as in everything, as befits Americans.

Yet this prayer addressed to a pulverized sky, this child,
This gristle and bone entombed in shards of words . . .
Reader, picture yourself under embery mounds,
Then be the furry expert, pawing and sniffing
Every ruined crevice to unearth what is human.

Just minutes ago raised hands were pillars upholding
The wordy authority of the authorized text.
Yes, this will be an issue in the election,
With no effort spared to find the two little arms
Of the one child left behind. (Shhh, a press conference,
A profile posed high on disintegrated brick,
An upraised arm silhouetted for *paparazzi*.)

Wood, nail, screw, socket, bracket, surely, that isn't
What the child is whispering? (Maybe he hears a niggle
Of digging, the faint whine of the back-hoe.)
Perhaps he's emitting streams of self-mothering, -fathering
As constant and disregarded as a heartbeat
Here in the margin that may have saved his life
As he ducked down into his dream . . . or maybe not.

At Hand

In the Domesday Book the wolves were summoning
The sheep to judgment, inscribing each piece of England
On sheepskin parchment, in red for headings, corrections,
Black for land, buildings, and chattel, each manor and barn,
Every hen was scratched in, every cock-
-a-doodle-doo attested and sworn to.

Today the notaries seem scarce as quills—
One or two peek from behind reams of 20-
Wt. bond at stationers', or walk out, blinking,
Hoover in hand, from the backrooms of mom & pop
Vacuum repair shops. Mr. Grossman (who tends
The "dragon" that snorts *in* hair, animal dander,
Dust mites) counters with sly courtesy,
"No, we're around, but we're not where we should be."
So, Gentil Knight . . .
                    In the backroom called the Past,
One unnamed scribe, his fingers gripping the left
Wing feather of a goose, which was also the king's
Property, moves the right hand he holds in fief
Across the parchment, which once clothed royal sheep,
Recording in juices from the king's plants
Every item encircled by the crown
(A king is all metonymy and commands
Encomiums issuing from the lips or pen
That the sword is mightier than).
                        Yesterday's quaint.
Today we're all conquerors, free to move everywhichway,
No constraint. Free to attend the hootenanny
In the theme park of Arden, warble off-tune and thrum
A chord for justice.
                    Free to roam the keyboard,
Prairie of symbols, riding the knuckles of "I,"

The fingertips that kiss the letters and numbers
Of desire: I input, I click, I drag, I frolic
In the puddle one-inch deep and a planet wide.

Tomorrow's the care of the State, which is avant garde:
In Liberty's bug-free, high-tech situation
Room, the oldest tool—hand with opposable thumb,
Heirloom from Olduvai—hovers as a hologram,
Anonymous index finger aimed at the naked
World, which is vertical, glowing, large scale, with zones
That soon will thrill to feel the digits of Freedom.

What Do We Learn by Falling?

Epiphany: Ptolemy's right, it's not *you* falling,
But the ground colliding upward, now the ice-
Jagged pavement itself is juddering under
Your motionless body, bloodying your nose,

Splitting your lip, at last it stops, and you're palm
To wincing palm with the boy who skinned his knee,
Yourself, but that odd impelled gliding of self—
No, world—is filed away as a secret history,

While you climb back to the life of geometry,
Healing and gain, which is *your* life. Rising again
Unsteady on the quiet ground. But a wobbly
Toddler inside you yearns for the outstretched arms

Of beginning and end, while do-si-do-ing a stumbling
Elder. *Nothing, little, a lot—all together.*
The two turn face to face and clasping hands,
Jig across every ruled line in the universe.

The Comforters admonish, Don't be suckered
By playing fields cantilevered over the Milky
Way. Old Ptolemy made frequent corrections
And watched where he stepped. Black ice is treacherous.

Early/Late

for Barbara Kinigstein

When the roofs of cars are themselves a fiery
road of spectral highlights and drivers
stick shadows on the empty street—
that early, the self might overflowing

meet itself coming the other way,
as once in a garden or mirror, but now
in the memory of a city of windows
each wider than its narrow house,

the inner life open for inspection—
upright comfort, sin swept away—
a shipshape city properly tied
with long and orderly lengths of water.

Somewhere in that city, but where
I could never be sure, is a miniature
of the city, reproducing every
bridge, canal house, and canal.

It has a life of its own, it lives
brief days and nights, twilights, dawns,
quicker than normal, nanoseconds
for seconds, and so it is older, older.

Meters for millimetres, a flying
object would shadow Regulierstraat
unidentified and a smaller you
cringing would encounter your own

finger, that's why it's better not
to meet oneself coming from another
dimension, to say, I could not find
the miniature and there is no doubling

of every thing, the wind blows
uniquely in its wayward way,
all the stick men enter their fiery
cars and drive them into the day.

Books That Have Read Me

And Chuang Tzu dreamed he was a book being read
by a character in the book he was reading . . .

Left open in a drizzle I was "unobserved"
On the verandah, my print joining with sky
By way of water and earth. Having just been held
In the palms of a "young and eligible girl"
While I "whispered betrayals" to her widening pupils.
Cracked binding of a life in Romanov Russia,
The elaborate samovar, the tea stains of boredom.
I, cloudy mirror weeping with my heroines.

[*Exit from* Uncle Vanya]

Brooklyn Academy of Music, 2/22/03

Now they're leaving us as the light
goes down and never goes out . . . Vanya
and Sonya totalling accounts . . .

Each night the watchman sings and the stars
descend to the fields—the summer is never-
ending—and cannot be counted. The trees

diminish from year to year. In a thousand
years, the happy people will never
remember us who sit breathless

before the applause begins, not wanting
this firefly era to end, its smell
of hay and tango of grovelling,

bang! of misaimed love and odour
of gunpowder rising like morning mist . . .
Telegin, play, we're perspiring, high

in the rafters, limbo's fellowship,
remembering how the doctor paced
out the summer a thousand miles

that way and this and sat in a chair.
There's no other way for us to be born
into pre-birth's motherland

where we were so bored oh god we put on
trousers and shaved, trying on selves,
slipped into dresses and tried devotion

or betrayal . . . it was always us
without Providence, dearest illusion, how funny!
bodiless souls taking pratfalls

or curling up on the table like cats,
lapping vodka as if there were no
tomorrow and tomorrow creeps in

in the dying clip-clop of the accounts . . .
We rise reluctantly from wide
Russia on the stage, a pin-

point of light now only a star . . .
We're leaving *them* for life in the new
empire and the prospect of war.

Notes

IRON PYRITES
The title is the scientific term for "fool's gold."

KEOLADEO
The title is the name of a bird sanctuary in northwestern India.

RAJASTHAN
The title is the name of a province in northwestern India.

INDIAN SUMMER AT SPRING LAKE
Spring Lake is a town on the New Jersey shore.

ROMA: SI/NO/FORSE
The title is Italian for "Rome: Yes/No/Maybe."

"ZERO'S AN AIR-TRAFFIC CONTROLLER"
Marco Polo Aeroporto is the airport that serves Venice. *Coppa melba* and *coppa bouffet* are ice-cream dishes advertised at the *Ferrovia Statione*, the "railroad station."

MAUVAISE FOI
The title is French for "bad faith."

THE GATES OF HELL
Tête reposant sur la main is French for "head resting on hand."

TELEPHONY
Trois milliards is French for "three billion."

STRINDBERG AT THE D'ORSAY

The title refers to an exhibition of paintings by the Swedish dramatist August Strindberg at the Musée d'Orsay, Paris.

HOPSCOTCH IN THE PLACE DES VOSGES

The Place des Vosges, a square in eastern Paris, was the site of Victor Hugo's apartment. The French words *terre* ("earth") and *ciel* ("sky") are the respective designations for the first and last boxes in the French version of hopscotch. The black stele bearing the Code of Hammurabi is on view at the Louvre.

ORIGAMI

The directions, in italics, are for the most part taken from *Complete Origami*, by Eric Kenneway.

AT HAND

The Domesday ("doomsday") Book, compiled 1086, was William the Conqueror's inventory of the "contents" of England.

EARLY/LATE

This poem was written after and—in a way not easily defined—in response to 9/11. One aspect of the doubling in the poem is the pairing of Amsterdam and New York (New Amsterdam).

Philip Fried's poems go extraordinarily deep, with such a light touch—BIG MEN SPEAKING TO LITTLE MEN is a delight but also a zeitgeist exploration of stunning originality and scope. Fried can move effortlessly from Victor Hugo to Freud, but there's nothing cerebral about the unnerving world he evokes, where "everywhere we go the chairs / worship in the empty cathedrals"; it's the world we've been living in without knowing it. "The Death of the Watchman," "Family Is a Stand of Talking Trees"—these are poems that define an arc, an ambitious engagement with the unknown. Fried's new book is a gentle but razor-sharp introduction to our new century. **D. Nurkse**

Philip Fried has the voice of an affectionate ironist and the wry ways of an urbane wit; but what Philip Fried also employs in this collection is an almost surgically keen deftness for giving us back the awful beauty of human circumstance. Some of the images here, quite literally, made me gasp with delight. **Phyllis Tickle**, compiler, *The Divine Hours*